GARDEN MAKEOVERS

Published in Great Britain in 2008
by John Wiley & Sons Ltd

Copyright © 2008
John Wiley & Sons Ltd, The Atrium, Southern Gate,
Chichester, West Sussex PO19 8SQ, England
Telephone +44 (0)1243 779777

Email (for orders and customer service enquiries):
cs-books@wiley.co.uk
Visit our Home Page on www.wiley.com

Other Wiley Editorial Offices

John Wiley & Sons Inc., 111 River Street, Hoboken,
NJ 07030, USA

Jossey-Bass, 989 Market Street, San Francisco,
CA 94103-1741, USA

Wiley-VCH Verlag GmbH, Boschstr. 12,
D-69469 Weinheim, Germany

John Wiley & Sons Australia Ltd, 42 McDougall Street,
Milton, Queensland 4064, Australia

John Wiley & Sons (Asia) Pte Ltd, 2 Clementi Loop #02-01,
Jin Xing Distripark, Singapore 129809

John Wiley & Sons Canada Ltd, 5353 Dundas Street West,
Suite 400, Etobicoke, Ontario M9B 6H8, Canada

Wiley also publishes its books in a variety of electronic
formats. Some content that appears in print may not be
available in electronic books.

Executive Commissioning Editor: Helen Castle
Project Editor: Miriam Swift
Publishing Assistant: Calver Lezama

ISBN   978-0-470-51762-8

Cover photo © Steve Gorton

Cover design © Jeremy Tilston, The Oak Studio Limited

Photo credits
All photographs by Steve Gorton unless stated below:
Pp 18(t), 68 (b), 69 (t l), 78 (b), 79 (t l) © The Landscape
Ornament Company
p 18 (b) © Mobilane (UK) Ltd
Pp 19 (b), 56 (t & b) © Garden Trellis Company Ltd
p 21 (b l) © Everedge
p 24 (t) © Blue Forest, www.blueforest.com
p 26 © istockphoto.com/dswebb
p 31(b) © istockphoto.com/cheng8
p 41(r t & b) © Elizabeth Fox
p 45 images courtesy of AHS Direct © Smart Solar Ltd
Pp 46 (t l) (r &b), 47 (t) © All Weather Lighting Ltd
www.allweatherlighting.co.uk, Design, Supply and
Installation. Tel: 01299 269 246
Pp 47 (b), 79(b) © Janet Korsak Coolscapes Ltd
Pp 68 (t), 69 (t r) © David Harber Ltd
p 69 (b) © Dennis Kilgallon, Kirkharle; Northumberland,
www.reddustceramics.co.uk
Pp 74 (b l), 78 (t), 79 (t r) © Alan Wilson
P 82 © istockphoto.com/Joss

Page design and layouts by
Jeremy Tilston, The Oak Studio Limited
Prepress by Artmedia Press Ltd • London
Printed and bound by Printer Trento, Italy

GARDEN MAKEOVERS

Garden Style Guides

CAROLINE TILSTON

Photography by Steve Gorton

Introduction

Sometimes it's really difficult to see what can be done with your own garden to improve it. Seeing it every day makes it too familiar, too entrenched in your mind to see how it might be different. There is help. There are some simple steps you can take to lift a garden, to titivate it and to transform it.

I'm not talking about huge building projects – there are lots of books out there full of intricate garden DIY jobs, packed with projects for people who know one end of a brick guillotine from the other. This is not one of those books. This is the book for people who think a G-cramp is something you get once a month. This book is for people like me, who occasionally get the urge to do something creative in the garden and want ideas, but beyond a pair of pliers and a spade we don't have a toolkit to call on or the wherewithal to use it. Basically, it's girly. Beautiful, girly projects that you can do in an afternoon and probably the most strenuous thing you'll have to do is shop.

However, these small projects, especially in a smaller garden, can make a huge difference. These little changes, which hopefully seem easy and doable one by one, will (or can) accumulate into a total transformation of your space.

There's one other thing which I've found with gardens – any effort you put in will transform it way beyond what the actual object is. Thought and time spent in the garden repays itself tenfold. You begin to see the space as yours and by adding to it, it becomes your space.

Outside rooms

It helps to think of the garden as an outside room. This attitude brings to bear all sorts of influences. Instead of being a place for gardening it becomes a canvas to decorate. You can paint the walls, put in new lighting, hang pictures, rearrange the furniture and in this way transform the space. You don't have to have a major overhaul to make a real difference.

So what I've done in this book is concentrate on the sorts of things I could do in an afternoon – or at worst in a couple of afternoons – to change a garden. No specialist DIY or gardening knowledge is needed. No special tools. These are fun things to do. My idea is that you can decide to do these on Saturday morning, maybe you'll need one trip to the DIY shop or garden centre and, after an enjoyable afternoon pottering, by evening time you can settle down with a G&T thinking 'that was a worthwhile thing to do'. There are a couple that require more planning but none which requires you to be a DIY expert.

This book is divided into two sections – Information and Inspiration.

Information

The first half of the book has10 chapters which cover 10 different ways to change your garden – from making special corners of the garden, to designing a water feature, to changing the lighting. For each approach, for each of the 10 chapters, I've included some specific projects with step by step information on how to do them.

1. **Shapes**
   To really transform your garden, transform the spaces you live in.

2. **Special areas**
   I think if there's one thing you can do in a garden to make it more captivating, it's putting in a den for adults and children. A space to hide away from the world and feel part of the garden.

3. **Paths & steps**
   People often forget, in the grand garden schemes, how they will move around the space, but paths are hugely important both for practical purposes and for their visual impact.

4. **Walls**
   In a smaller garden, walls can let the whole area down. Walls are wonderful places to exercise the quick fix – unify them and the space begins to look more defined.

5. **Lighting**
   Putting in lighting or improving the existing lighting can make a night-time garden romantic and exciting – it's another instant transformation.

6. **Colour**
   Paint is a fairly easy way to change the look of a garden. The right colour can regenerate a garden in a flash.

7. **Theme**
   A theme for a garden will immediately give unity to everything you do in it and choose for it.

8. **Decoration**
   This is the really fun bit – placing decorations on the walls, putting them on the ground, hanging them in the trees. If a garden is an outside room, these are the finishing touches.

9. **Water**
   Making a water feature yourself is probably a bit too much work, but you can design one and get it made for you …

10. **Projects for children**
    These are projects which children will enjoy … but so will adults.

Inspiration

The 10 gardens in the second half of the book are pure inspiration. To help turn that inspiration into action I've put lots of captions on the pictures and a plan of the garden to point out exactly what's been done, why it's been done and why the garden works. There are also 'before' pictures of each garden which I think are really inspirational – these give real hope for any disused, neglected space.

I hope that, by doing this, it will be easier to draw inspiration from the finished gardens and each of the features and techniques used will be more apparent for you to use in your own space.

Five tips before you do anything

You don't have to do this – you can just launch straight in and start changing the garden, but it might be helpful just to stand back for a minute and work out what you really want from your garden before you start. It may help you get the spaces right, the lighting in the right place and the whole thing working together better.

1. Consider the whole – even if just re-doing a little bit. How is it all going to work together?
2. Look carefully at what you've got and mark down what you like and don't like about it. Try to change or disguise what you don't like and make sure you keep what you do like.
3. Imagine your ideal garden, what is it about this garden that you like? Take inspiration from this, although it is probably not possible to recreate it wholesale!
4. Make a scrapbook of garden images you like, so when you do start to change your own garden, the direction is clear.
5. Think about how you want to use your garden – do you want it for dining, for children, for seclusion, for gardening even! Make sure that the things you are putting in are helping to achieve these needs.

Shapes

To really transform your garden, transform the spaces you live in. One of the easiest ways to transform a garden is to make the shape of the 'room' that you live in different. Most of us have gardens with ill-defined shapes. Mostly the shape of our garden room is the shape the boundaries give it, but change this – make rooms within the garden – and you will transform it.

Before these were redesigned the space of the garden was just the space within the boundaries.

After, there are exciting and beautifully proportioned rooms, with well-defined edges and interesting corners.

If you start to define areas within the garden's space – make rooms within the garden to live in – you will make the garden a completely different place. You create hidden areas and an element of surprise.

Think about making interlocking squares, circles, oblongs. Here are some possibilities for shapes within the garden …

How to make the rooms

There are lots of ways to make these rooms happen on the ground, some instant and easy, some less so. These boundaries or markers will define where the rooms are. Even something as simple as an overhead canopy can begin to give the idea of a separate space.

Walls

These are expensive and not the sort of thing to tackle on a Saturday afternoon unless you are very experienced, but they don't have to be very tall to make a division, even a wall just 30cm or so high will give enough of an implied division to start to make new spaces.

Planting

If you buy big plants, this can be an instant and quite easy way to make divisions. Something like bamboos placed in a line to make a kind of hedge will screen off and make an area separate. If they are large, the biggest problem will be digging the holes and manhandling the plants into position. Traditional hedges are the other possibility, but they tend to take time to grow up ... however ... you can buy instant hedge on a roll now, or try a 'green screen'. This is a wire frame already covered in plants, bolt the screens together and it's an instant hedge.

This green screen is from Mobilane.

Containers

Using containers avoids the digging work and if you get the nursery to plant the containers up all you will have to do is put them in the right position when you get them home. A repeated line of large planters will give a sense of enclosure to a space.

Two large pots either side of this bench, by the Landscape Ornament Company, help to define and enclose the sitting area.

Trellis

This is a great way to instantly transform your garden. It's easy to put up and can make walls and entrance ways in a flash. We're no longer bound by bog-standard trellis, there are slatted boards, wire trellis, panels with glass ….

With or without plants beautiful trellis like this one from The Garden Trellis Company encloses and divides spaces within the garden.

Step by step guide

Shaping lawns

INGREDIENTS

- String on a stick
- Spray paint
- Spade

Most gardens have lawns, and lawns contain the biggest secret of garden makeovers. One of the quickest and easiest ways to transform the apparent shape of a garden is by shaping the lawn. Make the lawn a good shape and you will transform your garden in a matter of minutes.

Step 1

Decide what shape you want the lawn to be. A strong shape like a square, rectangle or circle will work well. Circles are often the best way to give a more sympathetic, easier to live with, feel to the area.

Step 2

Use string and a stake to measure out the circle. Move the stake about and walk around a few times to make sure you're not going too close or too far away from any of the sides. If, to get a circle, you need to come away from one of the sides a long way, think about creating another small area off to the side.

Step 3

Once you're happy with the circle's shape and position, spray it out with paint or score the line into the grass with another stake.

Step 4

Use a spade to cut around this circle and remove the turf on the outside of the line.

Simply by shaping the lawn and filling in with plants, this garden has been transformed beyond recognition.

Step 5

If you want to make it look neat you can edge the lawn. Metal edging will curve round easily. This galvanised edging is from Everedge.

Step 6

Once the excess turf has been taken up you will need to put some plants or hard surface in the area that was lawn, but even before that's done the transformation is amazing.

Special areas

I think if there's one thing you can do in a garden to make it more captivating, it's putting in a den for adults and children. A space to hide away from the world and feel part of the garden.

This magical treehouse was designed and built by Blue Forest Limited.

What?

In any garden it's great to have a special area, a place just to sit and contemplate. Ideally it's hidden away, surrounded by leafy plants and approached by a secret path … that's not possible in many small gardens. But even in a very small garden there's usually room to tuck something out of the way, perhaps a seat that gets the evening sun, a hammock under a tree, or just the spot for a morning coffee – something that suits your lifestyle.

Size of the area?

This will depend on what you want to use it for. If it's a place for solitude, one chair will do, but if you want to be able to invite your friends around it's going to need to be bigger.

Why?

1. To give you somewhere to escape to.
2. To make the garden more interesting.
3. To hide parts of it and entice people to explore the garden.

Where?

This depends on what your ideal is.
A special area might be:

- Sunny or shady; it might be placed to catch the last rays of sunshine on a summer's evening
- Secluded or with a view
- Close to the house for convenience or as far away as possible.

How?

You will need to make both the walls and the floor of the area if they are not already there.

For the walls, to give seclusion …

- Using planting for the verticals will make it green and peaceful
- Trellis will give instant results
- A mixture of the two is ideal. Trellis for instant seclusion, plants for later leafyness.

For the floor

You will probably need some sort of hard-standing or it will be muddy and any chairs or tables you have will sink into the earth or grass.

One of the easiest ways to make hard-standing is with gravel …

Gravel

If you want to make a gravelled area properly you will need to:

1. Dig the whole area out to 15cm depth.
2. Put in wooden or metal edging to keep the gravel in the area so it doesn't travel.
3. Lay down 5cm of hardcore and compact it, with a roller if possible.
4. Put down 5cm of larger gravel or hoggin and again firm it down well with a roller.
5. And finally, you pour over 3cm depth of gravel and rake it neatly.

But I like quick fixes and you couldn't do all of that on a Saturday afternoon. What you can do, and I know as I made an area for myself like this in an afternoon last year, is a short-cut method.

The downside of this method is that it will start to look ropey after a few years as the sides sink – but I'll probably have moved house by then.

Weeds will come up but it's not a very big area and I just pull them out as they appear – you could spray the area too to help keep the weeds out.

All you do is mark out the area with string and sticks and skim 4 or 5cm of soil off the top and pour in the gravel. It is a complete and wonderful transformation, especially because your gravel will probably be light-coloured so what might have been quite a dark area now looks bright and fresh. To give it a bit more oomph you can put a couple of containers at either side of the entrance.

Step by step guide

Making a private seat

Ingredients
- Seat
- Planters
- Tall plants like bamboo

STEP 1

A seat against a bare wall doesn't look right nor does it look inviting.

STEP 2

To make it private and hidden away bring in pots of tall plants like bamboo and perhaps some lower planting as well to really bed the seat in and make it feel secluded. These tall plants are from R&R Saggers' nursery.

Paths & steps

P eople often forget, in the grand garden schemes, how they will move around the space, but paths are hugely important both for practical purposes and for their visual impact.

Putting in a path can change

- How a garden looks – the path is likely to give a strong line to the garden; it will divide the garden with lines and shapes at ground level.
- How you view it – if you have a path which you are likely to take, you will see the garden from that path. This will be your main viewpoint.
- How you move around the garden – your movement will be directed once you have a path and you are less likely to amble.

Creating a journey through the garden

A path going straight down a garden will foreshorten it and lead the eye right down to the end. This may be what you want to achieve if you have an over-long garden or have a focal point you want to draw attention to.

A meandering path will give a sense of discovery to the garden, especially if it goes right out of sight. If the whole meander is visible it will probably look a bit pointless, so use taller plants to hide the end of the journey and make it look like the path is curving for a reason.

TIP

If you want a curve on a path use smaller materials – from gravel up to brick – to get the curve. Otherwise you will have to cut slabs or have huge gaps between the stones as they turn the corner.

Lines of desire

This is a bit of jargon designers use to work out where to put paths in gardens. There's an old story about a designer of a university campus in America who left the whole site as grass for a year and then looked at where the grass had been worn out and turned to mud by the students' feet – that was where he put his paths. This story is used to demonstrate that you have to put paths exactly where people want them or they will not go on the paths. Children especially, it is said, will take a direct line and ignore paths unless you put the path along the shortest line between A and B. This is not true.

Children (and adults) will take the *easiest* route. If you block the direct route with shrubs and hedges the kids will go round them because it'll be easier to do so. You don't have to make straight lines for

It's human nature to make straight for a seat (or swing or gate), but don't let this dictate where you put your path.

paths – you just have to make the path the best option. You can have a meander but make the path curve around something substantial (this will, coincidentally, make it look better). The point about the campus was there was nothing else on the site so the shortest route was also the *easiest* and, to find out the most efficient way for people to move around the place, this was a good plan; but often gardens aren't about moving people about efficiently – all sorts of different values come into play.

Planting and water are excellent ways to make people take the scenic route.

Making paths

The easy, quick-fix way to make a path is to use gravel (see Chapter 2 on creating a gravel sitting area – the same ideas apply).

If you want to make a path over a patch of soil, you can also, quite easily, make a grass path using seeds or turf.

Stepping stones in a lawn

3

around the slab and take up the grass underneath; make sure the slab is going to sit lower than the lawn around it.

Ingredients
- String on a stick
- Spade
- Paving stones

Step 1
Take easy steps across the garden and mark where your feet fall. Count how many times you step – this is how many slabs you'll need to buy.

Step 2
Take one of the slabs and put it down on the first footfall. Use a piece of string and some pegs to get a dead straight line going from the side of this slab up to the end of the path.

Step 3
Put all the slabs in position and walk along the path to make sure the spacing still feels right, then mark

Step 4
You can put down mortar under the paving slab to help keep it in place, but you don't have to, especially if your soil is quite solid and stable.

Step 5
Cut holes in the turf for all the slabs and lower them into position.

Step by step guide
Pine cone steps

For each step you want to make you'll need:

- 2 tanalised (treated with a preservative so it is less likely to rot outside) wooden pegs, 15cm long by about a 1.25cm square
- Something to make the risers (the horizontal pieces of wood) – we used bits of old branches that were around the garden, but you can use planks or other timber. If you want the steps wider you will need longer risers. If you go wider than 60cm, I would put in extra pieces of vertical wood to hold the step in place.
- Pine cones or other material to build up the tread of the steps (can be shells, cobbles, soil etc.)
- Saw to cut up the wood (or you can ask at the builders' merchant who may be able to cut it for you)
- Hammer to knock in the pegs.

Putting steps into a garden can be a huge civil engineering project, but if you're sinking steps into a slope and they are only for walking on you can put in some yourself.

Step 1

Hammer in two verticals 40cm apart where you want the steps to go. These are to hold the riser so they should be slightly less far apart than the riser is long.

Step 2

Put the verticals and risers in for as many steps as you want to make.

Step 3

Fill up the space behind the new riser with infill – here we've used pine cones.

Step by step guide
Edging a path

Ingredients
- Spade
- Bricks

Half sink some bricks into the ground at the edge of a path or lawn to make a lovely, traditional edging.

Step 2
Put the bricks in at an angle.

Step 1
Dig a trench at the side of the gravel or lawn.

Step 3
Pour gravel over the dug area.

Walls

Walls are wonderful places to exercise the quick fix – unify them and the space begins to look more defined.

In a smaller garden, walls can let the whole area down – they are likely to be incredibly dominant in a small space but often they're a mishmash of different materials. If you can make them all the same or get them to at least look the same, the garden will look more of a piece.

In a city you are likely to have different types of fences or boundaries on each side. The idea is to make them the same all the way around. It's a bit like having a room inside where each wall has a different type of wallpaper. Make each wall the same and you will immediately give the whole place a more stylish, cleaner look.

The easiest way to do this is to face all the boundaries in trellis or battens.

Attaching trellis panels to existing fencing and topping off the fencing with trellis gives a whole new look to the area and increases your privacy. These panels are from the Garden Trellis Company.

As well as unifying the walls there are lots of enjoyable quick fixes for garden walls available now.

These horizontal battens, designed by InArcadia, are perfect to unify the walls and give the garden a modern look.

TIP

If you're going to replace boundaries completely, make sure they are yours – check the deeds of the house. If in doubt discuss it with your neighbour or just add a facing to your side of the existing fence or wall.

4

**Transforming the walls completely
changes the way a space looks and feels.**

Before

After

Before

After

Before

After

Top trellis tips

Julian Furness of the Garden Trellis Company has been installing and painting trellis for over 15 years. Here are some tips for installing and using trellis.

1. Horizontal battens are very popular now and give a clean contemporary look. Good design and quality materials will help them stand the test of time and not look dated.

2. If you want to disguise something, even a quite open trellis will be enough to fool the eye. Your eyes are drawn to the trellis not to what's behind it, particularly if the trellis is painted or stained.

3. If you want to fix trellis to a wall, consider the use of hinges, this will allow the panels to be opened away from the wall for maintenance.

4. Paint and stains will improve the life of trellis. Some good quality paint, if applied correctly, resists cracking and splitting. So if you do want to refresh it or change the colour, it can simply be a matter of cleaning it down and applying a new coat without the need to strip the old paint off.

5. If you're re-painting trellis, the easiest thing to do is to take it down and spray it. You'll need to hire a spray gun and have plenty of room to do this, but it takes the strain out of the job.

6. Try to avoid allowing timber to stand in water or water to stand on timber! Particularly watch out for any end grain, if these are exposed to water they will act like a sponge. Take extra care to treat or protect end grain more thoroughly and consider if drainage holes can be used.

Hang paintings or photographs on the wall

You can buy wonderful paintings to hang on walls outside, or you can get a photograph blown up and transformed into an outdoor piece of art.

This photograph has been enlarged and reverse-printed to glass for outdoor use by the Sign and Graphics Company.

ingarden have a great range of colourful prints for outdoor use.

This tiny area has been transformed by Elle Fox at Foxes Boxes. The walls have been painted white to lighten the area and smart new trellis all around unifies the space without enclosing it too much.

5

Lighting

Putting in lighting or improving the existing lighting can make a night-time garden romantic and exciting – it's another instant transformation.

I don't mean a security light above the back door, but really lighting it, to give the garden atmosphere – romantic, exciting and stylish – after dark.

Lighting is still hugely underestimated, it's the one thing I will bang on about to people I'm doing designs for. It's one thing which will make a huge difference, not only to how the garden looks but also to how you use it. People are sceptical about lighting – how often, they say, do we have evenings warm enough to sit out, even with global warming? It's a fair point, the trouble and expense of lighting might be too much for the odd time there's a balmy evening, but don't install it for summer evenings, install it for autumn, winter and spring evenings. So many of us have large windows overlooking the garden – from house extensions or from conservatories, and so few of us have curtains, there's the potential in the darkness out there to make a beautiful scene which will be enjoyed all year round – and that's even before you've managed to get out there for the odd late night dinner party or drink.

Obviously you can call in the electricians, dig up the garden to lay cables and spend a lot of time and money … but … for an instant makeover, candles, fairy lights and solar lights are ideal.

Solar lights

The principle of all solar lights is the same: there is a photosensitive cell which uses sunlight to power the light source. Generally speaking, the brighter the light is, the less time it will last, so they tend to be dimmer than mains lighting; but sprinkled through the garden, solar lights can make a huge impact on the way the garden looks after dark even if each individual source is not very bright. The way solar lights are being used is getting better and better with an ever wider range of possibilities. There are ones which fit flush with the paving, ones which float on water, and fairy lights.

Candles offer loads of potential for doing something that's easy but a bit different. Don't save these just for summer – in winter the effect of candles is magical. It takes a few minutes to light them, but it's worth it.

These wonderful solar lights are from AHS Direct.

4

1. If you have a texture on a wall – a downlight skimming across its surface, is a great way to make the most of it. This lighting is by All Weather Lighting.

2. Statues and urns take on a whole new look after dark if lit well. This urn is uplit with a spike light. This lighting is by All Weather Lighting.

3. Post lights at either side of the steps can work to mark the steps. This lighting is by All Weather Lighting.

4. These inset lights by All Weather Lighting are perfect not only to mark the step but also to reinforce the structural shape of the garden after dark.

5. A coffee table, a water feature and a light - this modern sculpture is by Coolscapes.

5

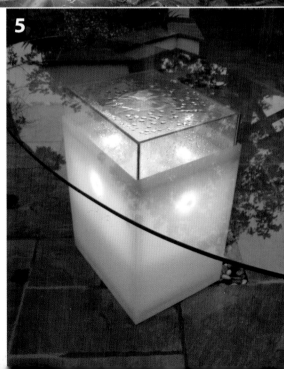

Jam jar tea light holders

Ingredients

- Old jam jars
- Thin wire
- Pliers
- Tea lights

Step 3

Drop the tea lights in and light them.

Step 1

Collect old jam jars and clean them.

Step 2

Tie wire around the tops of the jars and make a loop above them using pliers.

Chicken wire tea light holder

Ingredients
- Small gauge (1cm) chicken wire
- Coloured beads
- Gloss paint
- Jam jar lids
- Wire cutters
- Tea lights

Step 1
Collect jam jar lids, clean them and paint them using enamel paint.

Step 2
Wrap the small-gauge chicken wire around the lid and cut it to size.

Step 3
Thread beads onto the open wire and secure them.

Step 4
Wrap the chicken wire around the lid again and secure it by twisting the ends together.

Corkscrew candle holder

Ingredients
- Thick wire
- Pliers
- Candles
- Stick to curl wire around

Step 1
Use pliers to twist thick wire around a large stick (a brush handle is good) about the thickness of a candle.

Step 2
Slip the stick out and secure the wire to a branch, stick or fence panel. (Obviously being careful the candle won't set fire to anything above.)

Step 3
Put a candle into the holder and light it.

Fairy lights

Hung in the branches of trees and festooned through a pergola, fairy lights can be magical.

Use them as a light source for other things – filling up large jars or storm lanterns with the fairy lights.
You can also use them as a source of light for a more modern look …

Step by step guide
Chinese fairy lanterns

Ingredients
- 4 x paper light shades
- Outdoor fairy lights
- Broom handle
- Small nails and hammer
- Masking tape

Step 1
Twist the fairy lights up and down the broom handle and secure with tape or clips.

Step 2
Use nails and masking tape to secure the paper light shades in position up the pole.

Step 3
Stick the handle into the ground and bingo – modern lights.

6

Colour

P aint is a fairly easy way to change the look of a garden. The right colour can regenerate it in a flash.

Colour isn't something we use very much in the garden but it can have some quite startling effects. Bright, light colours will seriously jump out at you, especially at dusk. Dark colours, conversely, will drop back and disappear.

There are several ways to use colour in the garden:

1. To help unify the fences or uprights. Paint all the fences the same colour and they will look similar even if they are made of different materials.
2. To draw attention to something you want noticed.
3. For hiding eyesores. Painting things like ugly sheds in darker colours will help to make them retreat.
4. Colour used on different elements of the garden like furniture and pots will help to bring them together and make them look part of the same scheme.
5. To give colour in winter. Paint colour will be there all year round so can give a lift to the garden in winter.

TIP

Flat colour, dark or light, can make fences appear to jump forward which you probably don't want. It's better to have a stain that allows the texture of the wood to show through. The broken pattern acts like camouflage and the surface doesn't appear to be one solid colour.

Colour outside

1. Outside in the open air, colour can change enormously because of different light. In morning sun a light wall will look completely different than it does in evening shade, and this will alter again through the year as the angle of the sun rises and falls and the quality of the light itself changes.

2. The colour will fade over time, especially if it's in sunshine. You can use this to your advantage, choosing a brighter colour than you otherwise might to watch it fade and bed in over time.

The best thing to do is to go ahead and paint and see what happens, but if you're a cautious soul you can get sample pots and try them on pieces of wood. Leave these around outside for a while to see how they work in different lights.

Those paint swatch cards with their tiny areas of colour aren't very helpful when deciding what colour to paint large areas. I've painted a wall before and after I'd done it, I could have sworn that it was a different colour to the swatch. I've looked at the swatch and thought – yes, they've sold me a different colour, but hold it up against the wall and it *is* the same colour, it just looks very different when there's only a tiny sample and it's surrounded by white on the paper.

The best way of all to choose paint is to see it in someone else's garden or house. It's the best tester in the world. I've knocked on people's doors before now to ask and they have been flattered!

Tones

In lots of ways the tone of the colour you use is more important than the actual colour.

Every colour has a soft, neutral, more natural tone which will blend in with the garden in a classic way. These colours have more grey added to them and are closer to the original pigments that came from natural materials.

And then there's the zingy end of the scale with pure colours which will jump out and really have to be used carefully. These might look great in Morocco or Mexico, but in our dull northern light they can look garish and overbearing.

A grey/cream colour like this looks modern, fresh but not out of place. This trellis is by the Garden Trellis Company.

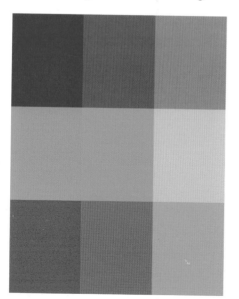

A colour like this, green/grey, is perfect to blend into the background. This trellis is by the Garden Trellis Company.

Theme

A theme for a garden will immediately give unity to everything you do in it and choose for it.

Themes don't have to be Disneyesque. They can be subtle and sophisticated – look at any well-designed garden and there will be a theme, a unifying idea, running through it. In these gardens the theme is often applied lightly and with a purpose so it's not just a copy or pastiche.

The list of themes or inspirations is endless, but once you have your theme you can begin to work out ways to build up the garden along the right lines. Plant some hedges, choose flowers in the same colour, get ornaments in the same vein. It sounds nebulous but an afternoon spent deciding on a theme or look for the garden will transform both how you look at the garden and how the garden will look.

7

With strongly coloured walls and clean lines, you might find inspiration from artists or well-known garden designers like Mexican architect, Luis Barragán.

A gravel garden can be turned into a seaside – an inspired one with bits of flotsam and jetsam. Driftwood sculptures, upturned sleepers to look like groynes, shells: all will help to give the feel of a seaside garden.

Or inspiration can come from a famous garden such as Sissinghurst, with a strong structure but feminine feel and single colour for the flowers.

It may come from a country. Here Morocco is the inspiration for a garden with clean rendered walls and cool falls of water.

Sculpture from foreign lands is a way to bring life to a garden and make it personal to you.

Step by step guide

Japanese-style decoration

Ingredients
- Slates, tiles, bricks or cobbles

Japanese designs have inspired many gardens or elements of gardens. An easy way to bring a Japanese touch to the garden is to use pebbles to make sculpture or use gravel to form patterns.

You can make a Japanese-inspired spiral on the ground quite easily. It works well if it's on a gravelled area. This is the sort of project that's great if you happen to have a lot of slates, roof tiles, bricks or cobbles hanging around (and if you've had your roof re-tiled you may have). But even if you don't have them around, you can buy them in specially.

Step 1

Choose the area where you'd like the sculpture – a place where it can be viewed easily but not walked on or tripped over.

Step 2

It's easy to break the tiles using a brick.

Step 3

Start to construct your spiral working from the centre outwards.

Seaside inspiration — windbreak

Ingredients

- Strong material
- Large eyelets
- String
- Brush handles
- Saw to make a notch in the brush handle

This windbreak will add to a seaside theme in the garden and give a sense of enclosure to an area. The same technique can be used to make an overhead sunshade or a tent.

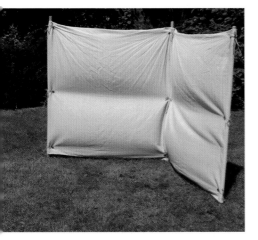

Step 1
Knock the eyelets into the corner of the material.

Step 2
Make a notch in the top of the brush handle so the string doesn't fall down.

Step 3
Use the string to thread through the eyelets and onto the posts and put the posts in the ground.

Decoration

This is the really fun bit – placing decorations on the walls, putting them on the ground, hanging them in the trees. If a garden is an outside room, these are the finishing touches.

Decoration tends to be downgraded in gardens, it's seen as an afterthought, something frivolous and not part of the design, but it can give life and spirit to a garden in a way which nothing else can. It can make the garden yours and imbue it with personality and life. So these things are important – but fun.

The Internet and garden centres are filled with statuary and wind chimes, wall hangings and arches. Any of these will do, but there is something even more special about making your own decorations, putting something of yourself into a garden. To decide what to put in the garden it does help to have a theme, an overall idea to help you choose which decorations will work.

Ideally decorations will, as well as looking good, serve a purpose. This is the great secret of getting things to look right. If the decoration has a purpose it will look like it was meant to be there.

You can:
- Finish off a view with an ornament
- Put urns at either side of an entrance
- Use a water feature as the centre point to an area
- Put an arch over a sculpture or decorative pot to frame it.

Alternatively if you can't think of a use for something, you can always hide it in the foliage as something to be stumbled across and admired, without any pretensions of impinging on the garden's design.

8

1. To get the perfect place for sculpture, they say, you can either seek high and low to find exactly the right piece to fit your garden or you can choose something that appeals and work your garden around it. Here the setting has been designed around the sculpture by David Harber. The piece, called 'The Portal', has in effect been given its own room in the garden with an avenue of trees as an entrance which is in keeping with its scale.

2. Sculpture can be interesting, fun and beautiful; these walnuts scattered across a field are from the Landscape Ornament Company.

3. A little touch like this plaque with a daffodil design from the Landscape Ornament Company can give added interest to even the smallest area.

4. A bold piece like this has enough weight and height to act as the centrepiece to the area. This armillary by David Harber is made of bronze and sits on a stone plinth.

5. Using sculpture to challenge your sense of scale works well in gardens. This ceramic piece is by Dennis Kilgallon of Red Dust Ceramics.

Planting pockets in lawn

Ingredients
- Bricks
- Spade
- Plant

This is a great way to disguise lawn that's not doing too well – perhaps because it's shady. It can also add interest and structure to an open piece of lawn by putting several of these in a staggered line.

Step 1
Decide where you would like to put the planting pockets – this may be to make a pattern on the lawn, or to direct people to one side, or just to hide a really ropey bit of grass.

Step 2
Mark out the size of the hole you will need by laying the bricks in position and scoring the grass around them.

Step 3
Dig a square hole out – deeper in the centre where the plant will go.

Step 4
Try the plant out – put it in position to make sure the hole is the right depth and it looks good.

Step 5
Carefully place the bricks back around the plant.

Step by step guide
Eucalyptus heart

Ingredients
- Eucalyptus stems – either from a florist or direct from a tree
- Thick wire for body
- Thin string to tie eucalyptus in
- Pliers

Step 2

Tie the eucalyptus into the heart using thin string.

Step 3

Hang in a window or over a seating area outside.

This is a variation of a wreath but rather than season-specific this will do for any time of year and should last; the eucalyptus will stay fresh. You can also use stems of box, but you will need more of these and so it will take a little longer. You can use the same technique to make spring bouquets with blossom and leaves or a heart from summer flowers, although obviously these won't last as long. Stick to smaller leaves, smaller flowers to get a cutesy effect. If you use holly, pine cones or sheaths of corn, the heart shape has to be much

bigger and it all gets a bit out of control.

If you use eucalyptus that's been dipped in glycerine it will last longer.

Step 1

Use the pliers to cut and form a heart shape from the thick wire, curl the two ends together, and with the ends of the wire make a hanging loop.

Water

M aking a water feature yourself is probably a bit too much work, but you can design one and get it made for you …

Water in the garden can make such a difference – it gives movement, sound and a focal point and centrepiece that nothing else can match.

There are plenty of off-the-peg water features available, there are lions' heads and cubes of granite, ones with water falling over leaves and sprinkling out of bird baths. Choosing and installing one of these can be enough to completely transform your space.

But none of them is quite unique. Why not design your own water feature and have it made for you?

Most water features boil down to a pump to lift the water up and a sump or reservoir to hold the water – the rest is decoration. How the water falls down, where the sump is and what it looks like, and the background, are all up for grabs. Why not experiment with how you would like your water feature to look, and then get an expert in to make the decorative bits.

- A metal fabricator can make something out of metal.
- A fibreglass manufacturer can make fibreglass to appear different colours and make moulds of pretty much any shape you want.
- Anything from stones, walls, bricks and a garden contractor can help you.

Once you've got your design and someone to help you make the exterior, you can get a lot of help on which pump and pipes you will need from the companies that supply them.

A shimmering water feature like this can bring light and life into a below-ground space. This lazy 's' -shaped stainless-steel water feature is by Alan Wilson.

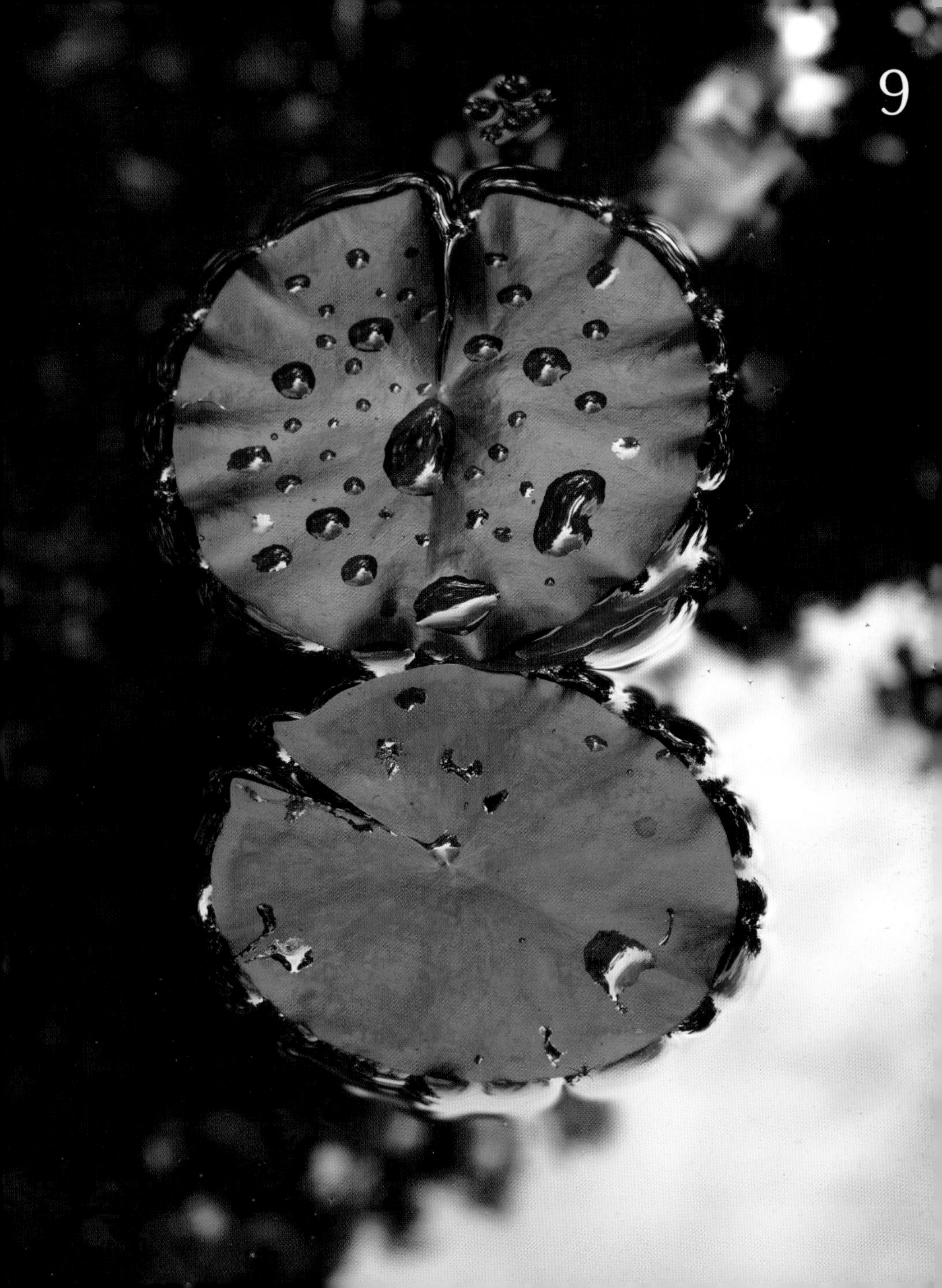

10 tips

1. The further up the water has to travel, the bigger the pump will be and the bigger the reservoir will be.

2. When the pump is turned off think about where the water in the whole system will go.

3. The suppliers of water feature components will be happy to help you get the right equipment for your project.

4. If you need a sheet of water falling down over a wide lip, you will need a reservoir behind the opening so the water can tip out evenly. This will mean there needs to be space behind the opening, so it can't be flush against a solid wall.

5. If the water is going to fall a long way it's likely to go all over the place. If you are having a sheet of water it won't stay as a sheet as it falls. It's much better to use something like Perspex or wires to guide the water and keep it in the system.

6. Water features are great when lit. Light through the water or go from under the water for the best results.

7. Once you know this it's really obvious but it's surprising how it catches people out … you don't need a source of water for a water feature – they are closed systems and only need topping up once in a while. You will need a source of electricity if you have a pump, lights or a filter.

8. For pumps and for lights get a qualified electrician in.

9. If the electricity needs to go a long way down the garden you may need to dig trenches and sink ducting into the ground which may cause disruption.

10. If all of that seems too much like hard work, think about a solar pump. These are now available for water features although they have obvious drawbacks (if it's dull they won't work, they will run out of puff after a while, they can only take water up a short way and the panel needs to be accommodated). They will avoid all the problems of getting electricity to a far-flung part of the garden.

This is a really simple but beautiful water feature. The shell was made by EGM UK from fibreglass. The container can be made in pretty much any size you want and any colour.

1. Don't be afraid to put something modern in a traditional setting. This modern piece by Alan Wilson sets off the surroundings.

2. This wall mask and shell basin can add a touch of gothic to the garden. They are from the Landscape Ornament Company.

3. Appearing to float on water, this water lily fountain from the Landscape Ornament Company combines traditional and modern.

4. Enclosed and framed by two containers this water feature, by Alan Wilson, has been designed into the garden.

5. At night water features with lighting come into their own, this coffee table is by Coolscapes.

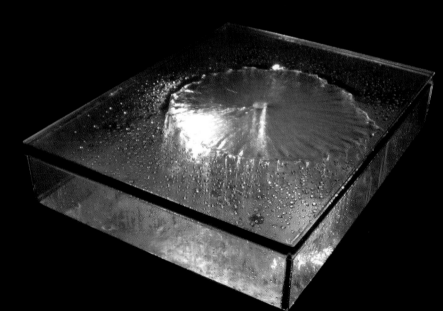

Projects for children

These are projects which children will enjoy … but so will adults.

Projects for children rarely turn out exactly as you'd planned, but always remember it's the doing that's important and not the end results. The good news about garden projects: at least you're outside so any mess is easier to deal with.

Step by step project
A mini herb garden

This is a great way to start children off with seeds and to help them notice the way they grow into plants, with different shaped leaves.

Ingredients
- Egg box
- Cleaned half egg shells
- Cotton wool
- Herb seeds

Step 3
Water the cotton wool carefully – normally you'd water after the seeds are sown, but in this small space children are likely to whoosh the seeds right out.

Step 4
Sprinkle the seeds on top.

Step 5
Put the box on a sunny window and keep lightly watered until the plants are big enough to use or be transplanted.

Step 1
Collect six clean half egg shells and an egg box.

Step 2
Fill the egg shells carefully with cotton wool.

A target

Not only is this fun to make, it's great for garden games afterwards and won't ruin the look of your garden. The circles can be used to shoot arrows or throw balls through.

Ingredients
- Bendy sticks or strips of bark (taken from deadwood)
- Wire
- Pliers

Step 1
Collect the strips of bark or twigs.

Step 3
Tie the circles together and then tie the whole thing to a tree with wire.

Step 2
Bend them into circles and tie them up with wire.

Inspiration

I love garden makeovers. They give hope to everyone. However awful your backyard or garden is looking – it can be transformed.

One thing these all have in common is that the boundaries have been changed or covered so that the walls of the new garden look great. As well as the boundary divisions, also look at the floors – if the floor looks good the whole scheme has more chance of working.

Thirdly, look at how the area is divided up – things aren't just scattered round, spaces are formed for seating areas, paths lead you through the garden. So the new designs help to make sense of the garden and how you use it.

In a final layer there are decorations, sculptures, water features and lighting. These are what give each garden its unique character.

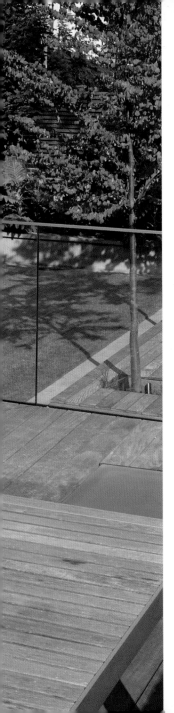

Terrace

One of the main problems for the owners of this garden was that it was overlooked from all sides. All around windows peered into the garden, and with a raised terrace coming from the rear of the newly refurbished house, the problem was acute – on the terrace it felt like you were on a stage where the whole world could see you. The garden was also a building site from all the work the owners, who run the architect firm Trevor Lahiff Architects, were doing in the house – it needed to be transformed and made private.

Before

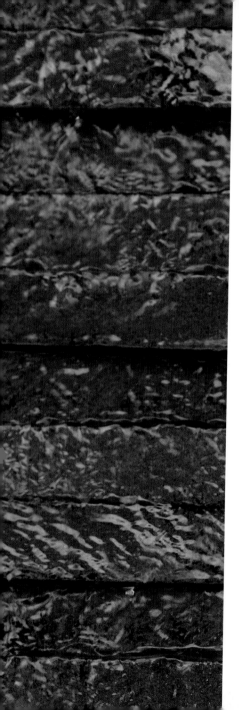

All around the garden James Lee, the designer they brought in, has built up the boundaries and unified them using sleek horizontal battens. On the terrace he has used very tall bamboos which instantly screen off the overlooking houses to one side. The other method of screening James has used is standard trees. These are bought from the nursery with a six foot high straight stem and the branches only start from this point up. So you don't use up precious space on the ground but you get screening just where you need it – above the lines of the walls. They also look wonderfully architectural with their strong upright forms.

As well as this screening round the garden, James has created a seating area with added shelter from the outside world. Standard trees are used around this inner area as well, and a huge water feature makes up one of the walls of its enclosure.

The tall trees are a great secret for an instant makeover. They are expensive but you don't need many of them and they give immediate height and maturity to the garden as well as screening above the line of fences and hedges.

Garden Plan

The influence of the far wall of the garden has been decreased by putting in a low retaining wall with greenery above.

At the end of the sitting area is a large water feature, so large it effectively forms a complete wall for this area, increasing the feeling that you are in another room here.

The lawn is surrounded by Chinese limestone edging to give it a really sleek finished look.

A line of a single type of architectural plants (euphorbia) has been put in to form the second long boundary of this sitting area.

A shady sitting area has been created on the right of the garden with an implied division between it and the rest of the garden by using a line of tall trees.

Three trees with clear stems along the wall mirror the ones used to enclose the sitting area on the other side of the lawn.

The raised terrace was already in place when garden designer James Lee started to look at this garden. The building had been completely refurbished and the garden had been used as the store yard and workroom for the house.

Toughened glass has been used as a safety barrier for the raised terrace to allow as much light in to the property as possible and to make the most of the views out to the garden.

Set into the wooden deck are frosted toughened glass panels to allow light down into the room below. They also act to give structure to the large terrace, delineating the area where the table and chairs go.

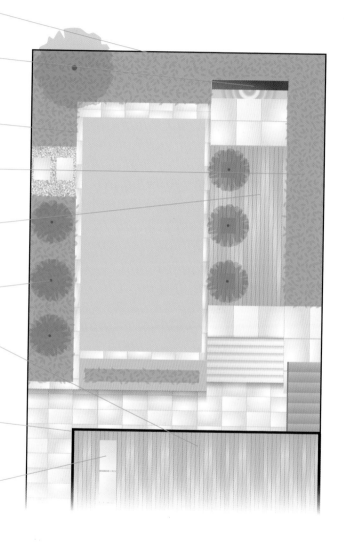

▶ The trees have been planted within the deck – a great idea to bring life to an area of decking.

▲ The trees in the garden were put in large. It is possible to buy trees like this, you ask for ones with a clear stem to 2 metres and you get this lovely, immediate, repeated upright pattern.

▲ The six trees planted are katsuras, with lovely heart-shaped leaves, great autumn colour, and when the leaves fall to the ground in autumn, they smell of toffee apples.

▲ Below the terrace is a raised bed which mimics the one at the rear of the garden. This one helps to break up the line of the retaining wall seen from the lower level of the house.

◄ The water wall at the end of the lower sitting area is designed by James Lee. Made of limestone strip cladding, the water falls over the jagged surface to a reservoir below.

▼ At the rear of the garden, horizontal cedar slats and a raised bed help to almost obscure the wall.

▲ If you want simple and you want style, use a single line of plants. Choose something like this euphorbia which will look good all through the year.

▼ Two distinct sitting areas, both secluded from the world, have been formed in the garden – one on the terrace and one in the garden below.

▲ The deck sitting area is raised above the surrounding Chinese limestone to reinforce the feeling that it is a discrete area.

▼ Neatly spaced planters containing huge bamboos fill up one end of the terrace and give instant evergreen screening.

▶ Lawn is a great material for an immediate makeover garden. If you use turf rather than seed, you get an absolutely instant effect that transforms the garden.

Level changes

This space was a depressing sight. The walls dominated an undefined open area and because you could see the high floor level from the main entrance, the whole garden felt like it was falling into the house. The steps were completely out of proportion to the garden and a potential disaster zone for the owners with their young children. So making the area more welcoming and making it safe for the youngsters was a key factor for them.

Before

Ruth Marshall from Cool Gardens has completely transformed the space. One of the first things she did was to plant raised beds across most of the garden as it rises up, leaving a gap to one side for access up steps. These planted beds soften the whole space and bring greenery right across the garden. The steps have not been put in line with the main entrance to the garden so your eye doesn't immediately travel up them and see just how high most of the garden is, instead it is stopped by the horizontal lines of the beds.

By narrowing the access way to the top, Ruth has not only enabled the steps to hold a baby gate, but she's also created a real 'room' up at the top with a feeling of seclusion from the rest of the garden. A built-in seat invites you to travel up to discover what is there. The steps, though narrower than before, are still wide enough to be inviting, and all around she has thought about the walls and how to deal with their dominance. She has used a geometrically designed trellis to top them off around the rear of the garden. This takes some of the height off the walls and also gives a unified look to this upper room. Down below she has chosen a wonderful sculpture which fits beautifully with the texture of the brick wall behind.

Garden Plan

Trellis has been used extensively in this garden to give interest to the high walls, unifying them and making the garden look finished.

Effectively two separate rooms have been created, a lower one which flows out from the house and an upper one secluded from the house.

Planters have been used to surround the upper area. Not only does this screen and enclose the space, it also means that you can't see how much higher the floor up here is when you look up from the main entrance. It's a small thing but it means your eye doesn't immediately register the height difference.

Low-maintenance planting of grasses and lavender has been used in the retaining wall beds.

The garden rises up sharply from the house in this typical town property.

▶ The raised beds to either side have been formed by concrete block walls, rendered and painted to give good, strong, modern-looking lines.

▲ The trellis for the garden has been specially designed to fit with the strong straight lines of the garden's design. It is traditional with a twist and provides screening while letting in plenty of light.

◀ The floor of the lower level is made of wood (western red cedar) – a great solution to raise the level of the patio slightly without the expense of bringing in hardcore, it also hides some extensive drainage works beneath it. Once raised, the inside and outside are at virtually the same level and there's an easy flow between the two.

▶ At the top of the garden a built-in seat has been created in a cosy corner. Set into the raised beds it forms part of the lines of the garden's design.

▲ Along the rear of the garden Ruth has put in a raised bed. This immediately cuts down the visual impact of the wall behind. Instead of seeing the wall from top to bottom, only the top half of the wall is visible above the raised beds.

▼ While the upper terrace is formed of stone, the steps have been made from wood. When changing the levels in a garden it is easier to form wooden steps based on a framework of wood, rather than trying to build up a base that's solid enough to lay stone on.

▶ Rather than have bare soil under the lavender, paddles (flat stones) have been used to decorate the containers.

Mosaic

The owners of this garden were gradually changing it into something they were happy with, they had already brought in Jano Williams, the designer, to make a natural-looking pond and then to redesign other parts of the garden. When it came to the area around the main entrance to the house, they wanted something different, and it needed to be bright and welcoming (before the area was drab and dark).

Before

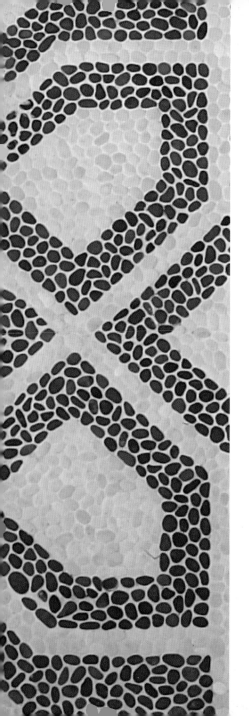

Jano has made a complete garden room around the entrance to the house. There is a sense of enclosure – with the raised beds curling around the seating area. The walls have been unified with horizontal battens and the whole thing lines up with the house. It is very different to the rest of the garden which has a more informal layout with sculpture dotted about. This is a piece of art in itself.

On the floor is a mosaic made of black and white pebbles, laid in a traditional geometric design. The retaining walls for the raised beds are creamy white and the planting is geometric and architectural.

The centrepiece to the whole area is created by two modern lights which have been built into a tall wall. Jano has used the same sorts of material you would find in shop signs to make glowing strips of neon bright colours that make a real statement for the area.

Garden Plan

Raised beds also wrap around the area to enclose it and make it feel more private.

A mosaic of black and white pebbles has been formed on the floor, acting like a carpet for the room.

Large upright cypress trees have been brought in to form an enclosure for the area.

The fence has been updated to one of horizontal battens which give a clean, modern look that is not too stark.

Set into the wall is a coloured light feature. Designed and made for the garden, it is more than a light, it borders on sculpture.

Structural planting gives instant greenery which will stay all through the winter.

▶ In the daytime the new area forms a retreat; its clean lines help the owners to relax.

▲ In the restrained surroundings, the bright colours of the light and cushions form a zingy contrast.

◀ Large fibreglass containers fit neatly against the wall to provide height and greenery where there's no soil.

▶ The newly designed area is all the more striking in its contrast to the rest of the garden.

Relaxed

Makeover gardens often assume the word 'instant', but just because we've got used to gardens being made over in three days on television, it doesn't mean you have to do it instantly in your own garden. You may want to take a more long-term approach – have a five-year plan.

Before

Gardens that are instant tend to have lots of hard landscaping – by its nature it looks wonderful the moment it's completed. They also tend to have minimal and regular planting – again the sort of thing that looks good immediately

If you don't want this, if you don't want concrete and stonework as the dominant feature, if you want to rely on a plethora of plants, how do you make over a garden?

The answer, as seen in this garden by owner and garden designer Ann Mollo, relies on two main elements. Have very wide borders, to stuff full of plants (and these will get more stuffed over the years), and secondly, make the divisions in the garden gently, without any sharp corners or visible lines.

Most of the garden here is filled with plants although a lawn occupies the space between the planting. You can see that this isn't a low-maintenance space! Basic principles of design have still been used – but they have been applied with a light touch and without the ruler-straight lines so loved by garden designers. At the rear Ann has made a separate space which cuts down the length of the garden. Within the part that's left, two areas widen out, again to make well-proportioned spaces within the long narrow garden. On top of this is a layer of ornaments, collected and placed over the years, and these now feel part of the garden.

Garden Plan

Through the central arch an obelisk, framed by the wood, forms a focal point for the whole garden. It needs the frame, without it, it would be too small to hold the entire space.

At the rear of the garden a separate space has been created to cut down the overall length of the garden. The space is created by three wooden arches spanning the garden.

The path is made of old red bricks laid in a herringbone pattern; this fits perfectly with the intricate intimate garden.

Tucked away behind the plants are secret seats for quiet contemplation, completely hidden from the rest of the world.

Because the surrounding trees and buildings cast a great deal of shade, the lawn doesn't do very well. Ann has taken out the worst areas of grass and put in plants instead.

Ann's garden is long and thin and one of the main aims of the design is to make the proportions of the spaces within the garden more pleasing. In the main part, the lawn gently curves in and out to make two rooms, each with good proportions.

▶ Three arches at the rear form a transparent barrier across the garden, the central one acts as a frame for a stone obelisk.

▲ This plant lover's garden always allows space for one more – and when even that isn't possible, Ann has brought in pots to accommodate yet more plants.

▼ Ivy and stone have an incredibly romantic feel to them – they conjure up old overgrown gardens and hidden places. Any stone will do – new stone will quickly take on the patina of age. If you want to speed up its decay, lay the ornament in long grass over winter.

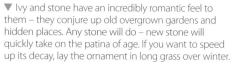

◄ Dainty plants line the edges of the border.

► An old seat has been left to blend back into the garden.

▲ Next to the house is a small sitting area. 'Nestled' doesn't begin to describe it, these plants are positively embracing the seats.

▼ I think this sums up this garden. Roses are quite hard work, they need pruning, feeding, spraying, tying in, but they are so beautiful, so romantic and when their buds are beginning to unfurl the whole world can be put right by their flowers.

▲ Mind-your-own-business –
a tiny-leafed creeping plant –
has been allowed to spread
through the brickwork.

▲ Hostas are perfect for this
garden. In winter they die down
completely, but come spring
their buds begin this incredible
display of perfect leaves.

▲ Tucked in every corner and
hidden behind every plant
there are ornaments and pretty
things nestling.

◄ Herringbone-patterned old bricks form a
gentle path. With no straight edges and a natural
earthy colour, the bricks and their pattern blend
in with the garden.

▼ This is definitely a garden for someone who
wants to spend time outside, watering pots and
pulling out weeds, but because it's not too large,
it is still manageable.

Colour

Makeovers involving a pot of paint are just perfect. It's relatively easy to do, it's relatively cheap and it can lift a whole area in a way that the installation of a single feature doesn't.

The bare bones of the garden were already in place but the space wasn't working. An ugly orange-coloured fence dominated the space, two huge trees stood out like sore thumbs and the whole garden looked sparse and utilitarian.

Before

Designer Charlotte Rowe has made some simple changes that really transform the area. One of the most important is her use of colour.

You may think this is a black and white garden (and I did too) but it's not. The fence has been painted but it isn't black, it's dark granite grey. The existing wall was stark white but is now painted a softer white with a grey hue to it. The planters are milky white. Pure black and white are too intense, too jumpy for our soft northern light, colours with grey in them (and that includes black and white) blend in better and look classier.

Using these near blacks and whites throughout has drawn the space together and unified it visually. The furniture has been chosen to carry on the same colour theme and to fit with the lines of the retaining walls. The deck, too, has been stained a darker colour to fit with the new scheme and to fit with the dark walnut floors inside the house.

The utilitarian feel has been banished by taking out all of the existing, quite dull plants and putting in block planting including shade-tolerant shrubs, grasses and perennials to give structure, rhythm and balance. They also break up the hard lines of the fence and retaining walls and hide a lot of the high fence. Extra containers and a line of polished black pebbles around the deck give the finishing touches to the makeover.

Garden Plan

The fence has been painted a dark granite grey colour – not jet black as this would shine out too much, the greyness helps colours fade back.

Statuary has been placed in the planting – it no longer needs to be big and bold enough to hold the space, instead it adds to the interest of the borders.

Filling the beds up with plants has softened the whole area. The box globes will give greenery and structure throughout the year.

It's a small detail but a wonderful piece of design. Around the edge of the deck Charlotte has taken up the decking and put down polished black pebbles. From a practical point of view it helps to keep the place clean (it's always these awkward corners of decking that get dirty) and tidies up any nasty cuts in the wood. Also, visually, it's a great finishing detail.

Opaque milky-coloured polyester resin containers continue the colour theme and also help to balance the garden and decrease the dominance of the boundaries. Previously the planting was around the rear – these bring planting towards the house and hide the bottom half of the fence on this side.

Carrying on the black and white theme, the table and chairs form an integral part of the makeover.

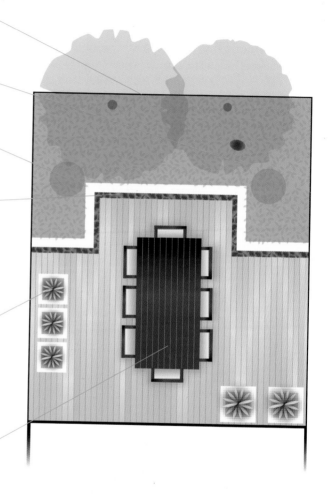

▶ Painting the fence has had an immediate and wonderful effect on this garden. It is no longer a space hampered by its fences. The fences form part of the stylish design.

◄ The statuary that previously was placed centre stage in this garden has been hidden amongst the foliage, to be stumbled across rather than admired from afar.

▼ The huge tree trunks are barely visible now against the dark fence. In winter time this view will not be bare. The bamboos will still be in leaf, the box balls will still be around and there's a line of yellow-stemmed dogwoods across the whole garden which will cut across the dark background throughout the winter.

▲ At the front of the house similar stylish touches have been applied, box balls in grey containers define the windows.

▼ Three polyester planters continue the black and white theme. Planted with swirling sedges they also continue the great contrast between slick straight lines and softer planting.

Contemporary

This small garden of a new property was so typical of the spaces left outside new houses. Dominated by fences and walls, containing nothing but some tired grass and concrete paving, the main view down the garden was of a fire escape and the back of a garage.

This is the sort of arrangement that faces many people when they look out of their window and it's really difficult to see how it can be made into something appealing, but it is possible.

Before

The first thing designer Denise Cadwallader from the garden design company, Garden Arts, did was to screen off the fire escape and garage door.

Next the main space of the garden was made regular using planted beds, some raised with retaining walls. These created a good square shape within them for the main area of the garden. The clients had decided that the space was too small to have grass and even though they have small children, they realised the children would gain more enjoyment from playing on a year-round surface than on patchy grass.

To one side Denise commissioned an in-built table and chairs from the Garden Trellis Company. Because they are built in and won't move, they help to reinforce the design lines and give dining space for the whole family without adding clutter to the garden. The materials used for this furniture and those used in the rest of the garden have been chosen to match the interior of the house. Dark wood, stainless steel and cream tiles are all used inside the property as well.

Finally, the beds have been filled with structural yet low-maintenance plants and a water feature added to give focus to the new garden room.

Garden Plan

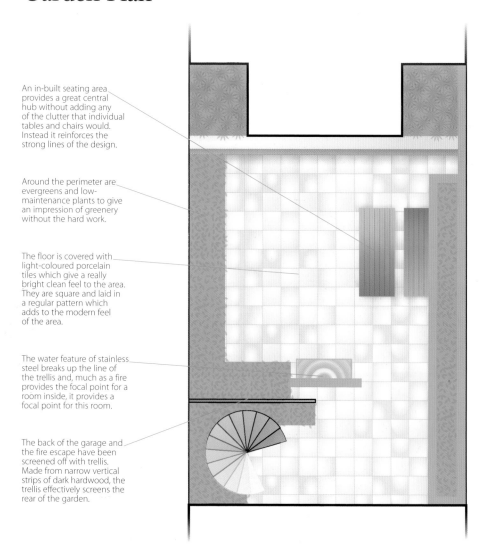

An in-built seating area provides a great central hub without adding any of the clutter that individual tables and chairs would. Instead it reinforces the strong lines of the design.

Around the perimeter are evergreens and low-maintenance plants to give an impression of greenery without the hard work.

The floor is covered with light-coloured porcelain tiles which give a really bright clean feel to the area. They are square and laid in a regular pattern which adds to the modern feel of the area.

The water feature of stainless steel breaks up the line of the trellis and, much as a fire provides the focal point for a room inside, it provides a focal point for this room.

The back of the garage and the fire escape have been screened off with trellis. Made from narrow vertical strips of dark hardwood, the trellis effectively screens the rear of the garden.

▶ Instead of traditional trellis, dark vertical strips of wood have been used to screen the staircase. Not only do these look modern and slick but they also make a really effective visual screen. The very tall thin plant is an Italian cypress, which keeps this skinny shape as it grows.

▲ The beautiful sophistication, simplicity and symmetry of the garden come into their own once the children have gone to bed and the adults use the space.

◄ The built-in bench has been specially made for this garden by the Garden Trellis Company and matches the trellis screen; it is painted with a stain called 'Jacobean walnut'.

► By keeping the design simple and the central area open, the designer, Denise Cadwallader, has left as big an area as possible for the children to play in.

▲ An awkward corner has been filled with a single large plant and instead of worrying about soil or underplanting, the area beneath has been covered with pebbles and stones to give an almost Japanese feel to this small space.

▲ The water feature has been carefully placed against a rendered wall painted a light colour (Dulux 'Buttermilk'), if it had been put against the dark trellis it would have been lost. The wall provides just the right-sized frame for its strong shape.

▲ The colours of the garden are incredibly important. The wall is painted a delicate cream colour, in the same tonal range, but just darker than the porcelain floor. This is offset by the darker wood of the table and the trellis.

▼ Evergreen box hedging surrounds the planting so, even in winter, there is a strong green structure to the garden.

▶ Pebbles are used at the base of the water feature. There's no standing water here so it is safe for the children. A light shines up at the water to catch its movement at night.

Water wall

This is a wonderful example of how precise, well-thought-out and well-executed changes can transform a garden. Charlotte Rowe, the designer, was called in to update this garden but not to change it completely.

Before

The major change she implemented was to replace the stone on the ground. Charlotte has chosen a much lighter stone, a Portuguese limestone, for its almost white colour. This light floor makes the whole scheme look more modern, bright and slick, but it is the detailing that really makes the difference.

The slabs are larger and less busy than the previous ones so give a smoother look to the area. The grout is the same colour as the slabs, again to smooth off the look of the floor. They have been laid crossways to widen the garden out, no longer are there straight lines going down the whole length of the garden.

The water feature has also been changed for something darker and more imposing. Sitting in the centre of the space, this new feature has the weight and substance to hold the entire garden.

But the water wall also works better because of a change you might not notice when you first look at the photos. It's subtle but hugely important. Charlotte has enclosed the water feature with planting. Box hedges come out into the garden to frame it. In doing this Charlotte has created three distinct rooms, three garden spaces. To one side the sofa now nestles into a sitting room, to the other the table and chairs are within the confines of a dining room, and at the centre the water feature fits perfectly between the two.

Garden Plan

The box hedges also partially enclose the two sitting areas at each end. They don't come out very far, but they don't need to, the implied division is all that's needed to make sense of the space.

The floor has been changed from sandstone to limestone. This is a good garden to look at if you're considering sandstone; it quickly darkens up to a dark buff colour. If you want a really light, clean and bright effect, a limestone will work better.

The slabs, larger than the original sandstone, have been laid crossways to widen the area so there aren't long lines leading down the longest axis.

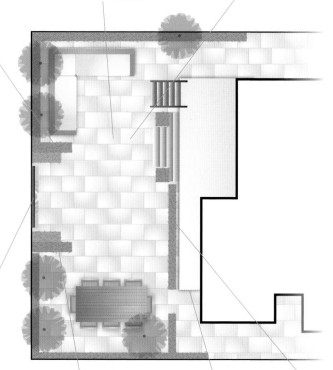

At the centre is a large wall water feature. There was a water feature here previously but this one is bigger and more in keeping with the scale of the garden. It rises right up to the top of the fence so there are no messy spaces above it.

Crucially, it has also been bedded into the garden. A surround of closely clipped box hedges has formed a frame for it so it doesn't appear to be plonked against the wall.

The low wall has been painted a light colour to match the paving below and the fence above.

An extra flower bed has been put in, again to provide enclosure for the sitting area.

▶ At the front the regular pattern of containers has been highlighted by uplighters.

▲ In the front garden a line of containers, picking up the white of the limestone, leads the eye to the side. Around their base a yew hedge gives definition to the edge of the border.

▶ The comfortable sofa fits perfectly into the corner of the garden. Snuggling in with the new box hedge to one side, it forms the ideal outside sitting room.

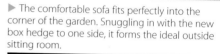

▲ The border uplighters shine through the planting to cast shadows on the fence.

◀ A beautiful detail in the paving: at the entrance to each of the sitting areas the pattern changes slightly to make a boundary – a subtle way to mark the entrance.

▲ It's subtle but it works. The planting has been slightly brought out to enclose the table. So the sitting area is marked out as a separate part of the garden and the table and chairs look like they are meant to be there.

▼ The Andrew Ewing water feature is uplit with fibre optics set at short intervals along the bottom of the wall.

◀ The water feature, a huge water wall by Andrew Ewing, is made from hand-hued granite.

▲ Olives are being used more and more in gardens, especially in warmer cities, but they don't like sitting in cold wet soil, so if you do plant one make sure the drainage is good, mix in lots of gravel so rainwater can drain away freely.

▲ Bamboos and box constitute the main, low-maintenance, planting in the garden. They form a green structure that looks good winter and summer.

▼ At night another aspect of the overhaul is apparent, a new lighting design. Lights have been put into the borders to uplight the plants and provide a subtle glow to the sitting area.

Plants

There were two main impetuses for the design of the makeover here. First, it had to be quick – the garden had to look good within weeks of the work beginning. Second, the owner likes plants and gardening and even wanted a vegetable garden.

Before

So the garden had to be full of plants but also quick to establish; these two things don't go together easily. Hard landscaping and lawns give the most instant 'wow' effect. Planting, by its nature takes a little longer to establish, but here the garden even in its first season looks great. So if you want lots of plants in your makeover this is a good garden to look at.

Emma Plunket, the garden's designer, has used standard trees to give instant height and maturity to the garden, elsewhere she has slightly overplanted so that, even in this, its first season, it looks full and lush. She has also used tall hedging plants around the sitting area to make an instant secluded room. These large plants are expensive but by choosing carefully where to put them she hasn't spent too much money and none of it is wasted.

Vegetables are great to give a garden a lived-in look, even in the first year, and Emma has put in a vegetable garden at the bottom of the plot.

But above all, and the most important thing in this garden to make it look good in its first year, is the really strong structure. The garden's design is made up of a simple but effective layout which, almost whatever the plants are doing, will look good.

Garden Plan

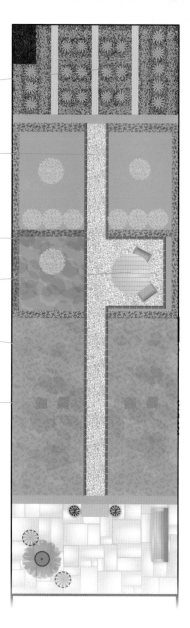

Right at the back, where the garden rises, Emma has formed a wonderful raised vegetable garden.

There is a long path going right down the garden, made of compacted gravel with an edge of reclaimed bricks, it has just the right mix of cottage garden and formality.

The path and the divided beds make for a very strong structure to the garden.

To one side of the path is a secluded seating area hidden away from the house.

Off to the side of the path are deep beds. In a garden of this size it's possible to fill it with plants and not be overwhelmed with maintenance.

Mature shrubs and tall trees have been used to give an instant effect.

▶ There is no lawn in this garden – the main area is given over to plants and vegetables. With careful choice of plants, the garden will look green all year round and will certainly, unlike a lawn, look different each year and look better as the years go on.

▲ Mixing vegetables, annuals, perennials and climbers the garden has instant colour which will get better and better as the years go on.

◀ Vegetables are a good option for immediate impact, they grow within weeks to cover ground and provide colour.

▼ Often it's the walls of a garden that let it down when it's first been done – climbers do take time to grow. Emma was lucky here – the walls are very attractive and add to the garden even when they are bare.

▲ The brazier is a perfect way to keep warm on colder nights and more environmentally friendly than a patio heater. This one is from the Internet Gardener.

▶ Purple and yellow make a great combination in the garden.

▼ Every space in the garden is filled up with plants so, even without a lawn, the effect is soft and green.

Vegetables

This is a very interesting option for an instant garden makeover. If you want one dedicated to fruit, vegetables, herbs and cut flowers, it's a great garden to look at. Although it will be a lot of work to look after, the upsides are enormous.

Before

The trick to making it work is the really strong design which will look interesting all through the year. Marney Hall, the designer of this garden, has gone for a formal, symmetrical layout using straight lines. It works very well. In the summer the formality of the design is softened by all the planting in the beds. In the winter the strong design shines through with an interesting structure, and to help it look good in winter there are evergreen plants alongside the paths to give all-year-round planting structure to the garden.

Marney has also put in a very strong central focal point, the raised pond. This is large enough to hold the whole garden. If the feature only consisted of the fountain it would look lost and out of place; with the large pond beneath, it is just right – there's a benefit to being bold when choosing a centrepiece like this.

Finally, around the edges of the garden are these enormous hedges, only put in a year ago! They have instantly enclosed the garden and given it an established air – a worthwhile investment.

As I say, the downsides of the garden are that it will take some looking after, but this is the sort of gardening people often don't mind doing and you will be able to feed your family from the plot!

Garden Plan

Right at the back of the garden is a greenhouse – at this time of year it's completely concealed by planting.

Evergreens spill over onto the path to soften it. Even in winter these will help to give greenery to the area.

A central focal point of a pond and fountain draws the whole garden together.

The arches are for plants to grow up like beans, peas, gourds and sweet peas in a random mixture, but they also give a wonderful sense of enclosure as you move through the garden.

There are paths down the sides of the garden to make access to the beds possible, but at this time of year, in high summer, the place is overgrown with flowers and produce.

Around the edges of the garden Marney has invested in tall (7ft) hedges and even taller trees to give an instant feeling of maturity to the garden.

▶ As well as herbs and vegetables, the garden also produces cut flowers.

▲ The pond is brand new but it looks like it belongs here. Made of stone and fitting perfectly into its allocated space, it has immediately taken on the essence of the place. It was made by The David Sharp Studio.

▶ Vegetables and annuals like this sunflower will provide cover and height in just a few months, creating an almost instant makeover.

▲ This isn't a low-maintenance option, there's a lot of planting to be done in spring and picking to be done at other times, and the greenhouse extends the growing season – and the work!

◀ This is a garden which will reward you with the fruits of your labours.

9

▲ These hedges have only been in this garden a matter of months, but because they were bought in huge a lovely mature arch like this is possible.

▼ Put a single type plant in a long line and you're pretty much guaranteed to get a beautiful, stylish effect. This is lady's mantle and is perfect to run along the front of a border.

◀ Fruit cages, made for the garden from hardwood, blend into the setting beautifully.

▲ Even before the full flush of summer the garden is looking wonderful – the strong structure of paths, the permanent planting around the edges of the beds and the line of arches give a completely different garden to that in the full abundance of summer.

▼ Earlier in the year the structure of the garden can be seen more clearly. Formal symmetrical paths run off the main axis to give access to the beds around.

Courtyard

The 'before' picture of this garden looks like a million other backyards. A few plants, a fence, it sits unloved and unused.

And it may have continued to be neglected except that the owners decided to put an extension onto the rear of the house which left what had been a small garden even smaller. They wanted something in the tiny pace that would live up to the wonderful new bright room they were building.

Before

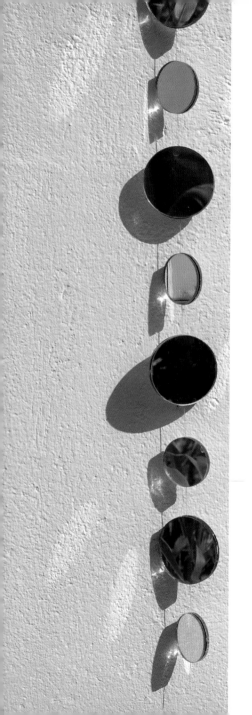

Rose Lennard, the designer they brought in, has used a simple layout to make the area into a usable outside dining and entertaining space. The fences have been replaced by white walls. Slate, to match the slate inside, now covers the ground and the area has been simply divided by a pool and an in-built seat.

The pool forms an L-shape around the house and extension leaving a square shape for the sitting area. To make the walls less dominant Rose has put in a great corner seat with a raised bed behind it which means as you look out, your eye is drawn to that and you hardly notice the high walls around the area.

This is an advertisement for looking at changes to the garden and house as one project. When the owners here decided to extend their house, they brought in a garden designer at the very beginning. From a practical point of view it saves time and money, the walls of the garden, the water feature, the flooring and the built-in seat could all be done at the same time and by the same builders as the house extension. Aesthetically there's a bonus too, the inside and outside both work together seamlessly to form the different parts of the same space.

10

Garden Plan

The corner has been cut off to provide a raised bed for plants with an in-built seat in front.

At the entrance from the sitting room is a water feature – water runs down a rill set into the wall, and then falls from a raised pool down to a lower pool with a walkway across the top of it.

The walls have been painted white and capped with lead to unify the outside area and join it with the new extension.

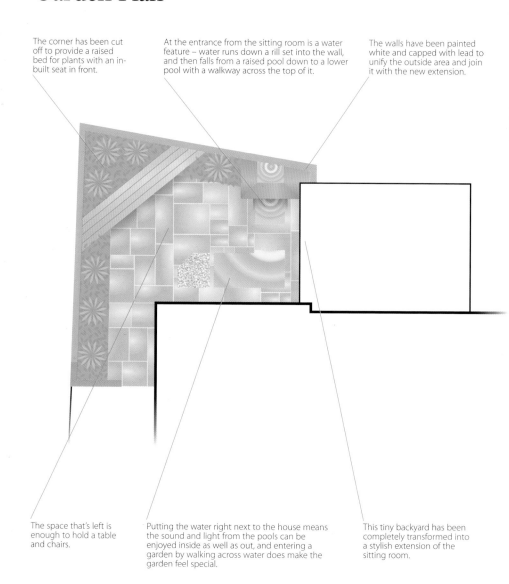

The space that's left is enough to hold a table and chairs.

Putting the water right next to the house means the sound and light from the pools can be enjoyed inside as well as out, and entering a garden by walking across water does make the garden feel special.

This tiny backyard has been completely transformed into a stylish extension of the sitting room.

▶ Having plants in a raised bed behind the seat is a great idea – it fills in an awkward corner and adds interest to the garden.

◀ The same burgundy and brown colours that have been used inside are picked up in the planting in the garden.

▲ In high summer the planting spills out from the beds surrounding the area to soften the design.

▼ The pools are lined with mosaic tiles. They are more expensive but if the lining is going to be on view they will look much better than a butyl lining.

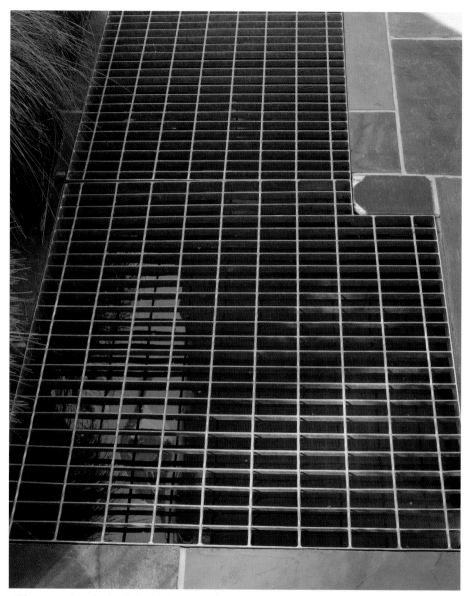

▲ The owners have had grilles made for the pools so that the garden is safer for children. The safest place to put the grille is above the water line, if they are below the water level they may be more invisible but there's still a possible risk to children.

▼ Evergreen low-maintenance plants fill the beds on either side of the garden.

▲ The smooth slate is darker than the surrounding render. This has been done here to create a specific effect and the lines of the render make an impressive pattern. More often you would want the render to be as dark as or darker than the stone, so it blends in.

▼ The courtyard outside fits perfectly with the interior of the new extension.

▶ The same riven slate has been used inside and out to give the feeling of a continuous room.

Directory

Products

AHS Direct
Garden and home
www.ahsdirect.co.uk

All Weather Lighting Ltd
Garden and outdoor lighting
www.allweatherlighting.co.uk

Alan Wilson
Contemporary water features and sculpture
www.thesculptureworkshop.co.uk

Andrew Ewing
Aquatecture
www.andrewewing.co.uk

Blue Forest
Exclusive Tree Houses and Eco-lodges
www.blueforest.com

Boldstone Sculpture
Wall pieces and water features
www.boldstonesculpture.co.uk

Cheeky Mojito
Outdoor art canvasses
www.cheekymojito.com

Coolscapes
Water sculpture
www.coolscapes.co.uk

David Harber
Sundials, sculpture and water features for the garden
www.davidharber.com

The David Sharp Studio
Specialists in reconstructed stone
www.david-sharp.co.uk

**Dennis Kilgallon
Red Dust Ceramics**
www.reddustceramics.co.uk

EGM UK Fibreglass Ltd
Fibreglass planters and other objects
01279 851 910

EverEdge
Galvanised metal lawn edging
www.everedge.co.uk

Foxes Boxes
Creative window box and balcony dressing
www.foxesboxes.co.uk

ingarden
Products for modern outdoor living
www.ingarden.co.uk

Insideout Garden Art
Weatherproof images to decorate your outdoor space
www.insideout-gardenart.co.uk

The Landscape Ornament Company
Garden ornaments with a difference
www.landscapeornament.com

London Reclaim Brick Merchants
Quality reclaimed bricks
www.lrbm.com

Mobilane
Green screens
www.mobilane.co.uk

R&R Saggers
Plant nursery, florist and topiary hire
www.randrsaggers.co.uk

Smart Solar Ltd
www.smartsolar.co.uk
Solar lighting available through AHS Direct

The Garden Trellis Company
Trellis and garden woodwork
www.gardentrellis.co.uk

The Internet Gardener
Online garden centre
www.internetgardener.co.uk

The Sign and Graphics Company
Outdoor photographic prints
www.thesign.co.uk

Trevor | Lahiff Architects
www.tlastudio.co.uk

Designers

Ann Mollo Garden Design
020 7603 3762
annmollogardens@aol.com

Charlotte Rowe Garden Design
www.charlotterowe.com

Denise Cadwallader
www.garden-arts.com

InArcadia Landscape Gardening
www.inarcadia.com

**James Lee Landscape &
Garden Design**
www.jamesleedesign.com

Jano Williams Garden Design
www.janowilliams.com

The Marney Hall Consultancy
www.marneyhallconsultancy.co.uk

Emma Plunket
www.plunketgardens.com

Rose Lennard
Chameleon Design
www.chameleongardens.co.uk

Ruth Marshall
Cool Gardens Landscaping
www.coolgardens.co.uk